CONTAINER GARDENING

Your gardening world may be an apartment balcony, a few hectares in the country, or somewhere in between, but all three probably have something in common: plants in containers. This hot new gardening trend can help jazz up a corner of a deck, add privacy to a front porch with a couple of hanging baskets, or be your entire garden — a portable, flexible method of indulging your green thumb.

Containers put you in the driver's seat: you can control the soil, water, light, even the temperature. In the following pages, we'll introduce you to the world of container gardening. We'll talk about design (both with regard to using containers as part of your garden plan and creating a well-designed container planting), review some plants that do extremely well in containers, explain how to plant a container and care for it, look at containers throughout the seasons, and give you some ideas you can follow or adapt.

TEN REASONS TO LOVE CONTAINERS

1. The containers themselves can be decorative — use them as focal points on the deck, the patio, at the front door, or at the end of a path.

2. The style of container you choose — from classical urns to found objects, such as old baskets or tubs — can reflect the style of your garden.

3. They provide interest throughout the year as you change the plant- ings to reflect the seasons.

4. They're an inexpensive way to make a house look special — for example, containers flanking a front door make it welcoming.

5. They are small-scale environments in which you can perfect your gardening skills.

6. They provide flexibility — you can mix and match plantings, test colour combina- tions and growing habits.

7. You can move containers around, changing the feel of the arrangement as often as you want.

8. You can emphasize the beauty of a single plant when it's planted in a container.

9. You can grow almost anything in containers: bulbs, vines, trees, vegetables, herbs.

10. They make gardening possible in difficult places.

Above, a classically-shaped urn is planted with fall beauties. Right, *the pink-flowered tropical vine* Mandevilla *'Alice DuPont' clambers up a support in the centre of this urn. Cascading over the edges is trailing pink verbena.*

DESIGNING WITH CONTAINERS

P lants in containers can help solve some garden design problems.

- Fill an empty corner with one smashing specimen in a container or a group of containers full of plants that complement one another in colour, shape, and texture.

- Camouflage bad views or features with container plants. Fast-growing annual vines such as morning glory can quickly scramble up a trellis, not only hiding an unattractive view, but becoming the focus of attention themselves.

- Containers can be used to add instant height to a bed. One way is to set a pot on another upturned pot, bricks, or wooden box to raise it. If the container plantings are spilling over the edges, the pot itself may not even be visible.

- Containers make wonderful design features and focal points. You can concentrate on showing off the container or its contents by setting it at the juncture of two paths, at the end of a walkway, in the middle of a patio — anywhere it will be the showpiece.

- Use containers to define space. Place them strategically to make a "path" or to enclose space on a deck or patio.

OTHER USES FOR CONTAINERS

- Take advantage of a warm microclimate — grow plants that need more heat and sun than you can give them elsewhere in your garden.

- Grow plants where soil is poor and digging difficult.

- Make a manageable garden for the elderly, disabled, and children.

- It's easy to reflect seasonal changes in colour and interest. In the spring, pots of exuberant pansies tell everyone you're ready for spring; in the summer, a joyful jumble of pots marching up the front steps welcomes visitors. In the fall, the emphasis is on frost resistance — use asters, mums, or kale for colour and resistance to Jack Frost. Finally, get carried away with winter arrangements: stark branches, voluptuous evergreen boughs, silver and red bows!

- The small garden, or even a property with no garden at all, is perfect for containers.

DESIGN TIPS

To arrange containers in a pleasing way:

- Group them in uneven numbers — three or five, for example.

- Use a mixture of large and small, tall and short containers.

- Break the rules when it feels right!

FRIENDS
OF THE MISSISSAUGA LIBRARY SYSTEM

Thank you for your SUPPORT.

This elegant urn is in keeping with the formal mood of the house.

PLANTER PANACHE

Whether you're setting out to plan a garden or have one that's well-established, containers can enhance your theme. Include them to carry out a colour scheme, to emphasize an entrance, or to act as a focal point. In the established garden, they can inject new life in a ho-hum view.

- Move the pots around for different effects, combining them with other containers or established plants.

- A grouping of terra cotta pots of different sizes adds zing to the edge of a deck, patio, or swimming pool terrace. Together, they'll make a bolder statement than if they're placed apart.

- The same principles of design apply to pots as to plants (see *Plantings* in this series). One important concept is layering — simply, it's putting tall materials at the back or centre, mid-size spreading or bushy plants in the middle, and low-growing or trailing plants at the edge.

- Choose the container to complement the architecture of the house, the colour scheme of the garden, and the space in which it will sit. It should not dominate or make the area feel crowded but neither should it be overwhelmed and lost amid other plantings.

Right, *Containers of different sizes, shapes, and textures can be grouped on a patio to bring the colour of the garden a little closer.*
Below, *An impressive collection of shade-loving coleus plants is shown off in a simple arrangement of terra cotta pots.*

PLANTING TIP

To make container plantings look well established, buy plants in 4- or 6-inch pots. They'll make an immediate impact. Interplant with plants in smaller pots.

LOOKING GOOD

D esigning with containers can be easy. Here are some quick tips to ensure success . . .

- Buy the largest containers you can — in fact, bigger than you think you'll need. Small pots dry out too quickly and there's too much competition for root space and nutrients.

- Apply the design principles outlined in our companion book, *Design*. Scale and proportion are important concepts, especially when a single plant is grown in a container. The container should not be so large that it overpowers the plant, nor should it be so small that it looks as if the plant will topple the container over. Look at the ratio of the plant's height to the width of the container. Although it's hard to give a precise rule of thumb for this ratio, a pleasing effect can be achieved by having the tallest plant twice the height or the width of the container. If a pot is about 30 cm (12 inches) across, the mature height of the tallest

plant would be 60 cm (24 inches). For a dramatic look, plant a single specimen as a standard in the centre of the pot using these approximate dimensions. A softer effect is produced by using cascading plants at the edges of the container.

- For an instantly impressive planter, use mature plants, especially those already in bloom. Cram in as many as you can. Protect them from direct sun and strong breezes for a day or two — they will show the stress of being transplanted more than younger plants, but they'll recover quickly and look like they've been there for weeks.

- For easier care, use drought-tolerant plants in your containers.

Left, A tender, orange-flowered abutilon pairs beautifully with trailing white bacopa 'Snowflake' in this stone urn.
Right, A whimsical iron peacock trellis entwined with white sweet peas presides over pink Mandevilla 'Little Red Riding Hood' and trailing purple verbena.

DESIGNING A BEAUTIFUL CONTAINER

- Choose plants you love and, as you do so, keep your colour scheme in mind.

- Vary the heights, aiming to include a couple of trailers and a taller plant for the centre of the arrangement.

- In the garden centre, gather together the plants you like and try them out before you buy them. Group them in a pot to judge their impact — in effect, put your container together on the spot.

- Buy plants in 4- or 6-inch pots. They'll be sufficiently mature to give your container a lush full look — much more satisfying than waiting half the summer for smaller plants to get over their transplant shock and begin to put on growth.

- Choose a container appropriate to your house and garden style — romantic, formal, architectural, cottagey, and so forth.

SOME GREAT COLOUR COMBOS

- silver, pink, and blue
- yellow, orange, and red
- silver, yellow, and blue

A handsome and unusual carved stone pot is the perfect container for a stunning fall arrangement of purple and white ornamental kale and delicate mauve asters.

SOME GREAT PLANT COMBOS

- 'Purple Wave' petunias and helichrysum at the base of a fuschia standard or pink hibiscus standard for pretty purple, pink, and silver colour scheme

- a hot combination: orange or red canna lily, red geraniums, orange and yellow nonstop begonias, with the trailer 'Blackie' potato vine

- purple lobelia ('Lilac Cascade' or 'Blue Splash'), helichrysum, white geranium, orange zinnia (*Zinnia angustifolia*), and butter daisy (*Melampodium paludosum*), which has deep yellow flowers

This beautiful container, planted in tones of pink like the garden, is a stunning focal point.

CONTAINER MATERIALS

You can grow plants in just about anything as long as it will hold sufficient soil and water. Ideally, the container should have a hole in the bottom for drainage but don't pass up a beautiful container just because it doesn't have a drainage hole.

TERRA COTTA

- You can't go wrong with terra cotta, a traditional material for containers. The pots are unglazed clay, porous, and rusty red in colour.

- These pots are available in a variety of sizes. The small ones are relatively cheap; large pots in high-quality clay can be very expensive. Some are plain, some are decorated but all show plants off to perfection.

- Advantages: Moderately inexpensive; useful in any garden style; long-lasting if handled with some care; fairly lightweight, depending on size; allows roots to breathe so plants are healthy.

- Disadvantages: Breakable; needs special winter care.

- Winter care: Empty soil and store upside down in a protected spot. Due to winter's freeze-thaw cycle, terra cotta pots will crack if left outdoors with soil in them.

Right, The edges of the wooden container are softened by trailing plants. Below, an elegant blue-glazed clay pot has been left standing empty to make a dramatically simple design statement in the garden

GLAZED CLAY

- Pots made with glazed surfaces will not dry out as quickly as terra cotta.

- These pots might not have a drainage hole but you can set other pots, with drainage holes, inside them.

- Advantages: Retains moisture longer than terra cotta; fairly lightweight; more decorative as a garden accessory, can carry out colour themes.

- Disadvantages: Can be expensive; breakable.

- Winter care: Store in protected spot after emptying the soil.

WOOD

- Wood containers are generally easy-care and no-fuss, and come in a wide variety of styles.
- Paint or stain wood to match house trim or to reflect colour schemes.
- The best woods are redwood and cedar, longlasting woods that weather to a lovely grey with no painting or preservatives needed. Pressure-treated wood lasts a long time, but should not be used for containers in which herbs or vegetables are grown.
- Advantages: Fairly inexpensive; can be constructed to any shape or size; offer good root insulation.
- Disadvantages: Poorly constructed wood containers may eventually fall apart; once you start painting, you need to keep them painted.
- Winter care: Can be left outdoors all year long.

PLASTIC

- Don't turn your nose up at plastic! There are many types of plastic on the market today. Strong resin pots are virtually indistinguishable from terra cotta or stone, come in attractive colours, and are resistant to ultraviolet rays.
- Advantages: Lightweight; holds moisture well.
- Disadvantages: May deteriorate in the sun after a few years.
- Winter care: Most plastic containers withstand cold winter temperatures and do not need to be emptied in fall.

CAST IRON

- For the elegant garden, there's nothing to match a sophisticated cast iron container.
- A true all-season container, cast iron earns its keep throughout the year. For a classic look, decorate with evergreen boughs in the winter; insert a few branches of the bittersweet vine, dogwood, or highbush cranberry for added colour.
- Paint cast iron with a verdigris paint to dress it up.
- Advantages: Its weight makes it burglar-proof; holds moisture well; can be left outside all winter.
- Disadvantages: Heavy; can be expensive.

CONCRETE AND STONE

- From simple modern lines to the ornate, there's a concrete or stone container to fit the style of your garden.
- Advantages: available in many shapes and styles, retains warmth and moisture, and is slow to react to temperature changes; low maintenance; can be aged with moss.
- Disadvantages: heavy; moderate to very expensive, depending on quality or age.

Right, A cast iron urn bears a hot-coloured profusion of pink geraniums, orange tuberous begonias and pink portulaca. Below, A cloud of easy-care cascading (or balcon) geraniums in shades of pink enhances the blue-gray colour of the brick pedestal.

SPECIAL CONTAINERS

WINDOW BOXES

Most modern houses aren't built with the deep, sturdy windowsills of French farmhouses and English cottages — but you can still grace your windows with the lush colourful tumble we associate with European window boxes.

LOCATION

- Situate the boxes where they will be easy to water.
- If you haven't got windowsills, install a shelf below the window and place the box on it.

MATERIALS

- Wood is a good material for window boxes. It can be painted the same colour as the trim of the window.
- Terra cotta makes an exceptional window box, giving a natural look and allowing roots to breathe.
- Sturdy plastic makes a good alternative. It's light in weight and will hold moisture well.

WATERING REQUIREMENTS

- Window boxes situated under house eaves will not be exposed to rain and will require regular watering.
- In a hot or sunny location, window boxes need watering daily.

Pretty flowers tumbling over the edge of a windowbox adds a romantic touch to the face of a house

HANGING BASKETS

Front porches and hanging baskets — a charming combo! But hanging planters are not always easy to maintain successfully. They tend to dry out more quickly than any other type of container, and large ones can be quite heavy, especially when just watered.

LOCATION

- We've already mentioned porches, but there are many other places you can hang baskets: from any overhead beam, from a hook attached to a wall, or from a free-standing pole.

- Sun or shade is no problem — just choose your plants accordingly (see pages 28 to 35).

A large hanging basket filled with pink ivy geraniums and tiny yellow Dahlberg daisies (Dyssodia tenuiloba) *creates a lovely view through this window.*

MATERIALS

- Wire baskets lined with sphagnum moss have traditionally been used for hanging baskets. Using a synthetic moss-like liner updates them while maintaining their natural look.

- Cocoa fibre inserts fit inside wire baskets. They make a neat alternative to moss and conserve moisture.

- Fibre containers are a great way to exhibit plants and to hold moisture.

WATERING REQUIREMENTS

- Watering daily is vital for plants in moss-lined wire hanging baskets.

- If your hanging baskets are difficult to reach, buy a wand attachment for your garden hose or install a pulley arrangement to raise and lower the baskets.

- If the soil in the basket has become quite dry, water will often roll off the crust that forms. Lower the basket into a pail or basin of water, ensuring that at least the bottom third of the basket is in the water. Leave it for several hours to soak up the moisture. Remove the basket and let it drain before returning it to its spot.

HOW TO PLANT CONTAINERS

SOIL MIXES

The soil and amendments you use are extremely important — container growing is intensive growing. The soil needs to deliver lots of nutrients and moisture to the plants all season long.

- Purchase a ready-mixed soil specially formulated for containers. PC Magic Planter Soil, for example, is great for containers — it contains bentonite clay, which helps store water, as well as slow-release fertilizers that last through the season.

- Add a slow-release fertilizer to the soil just before you plant if the soil mixture does not have added fertilizers.

PLANTING

- With the plants still in their original pots, arrange them on your work space in the configuration you want to plant them.

- Cover the container's drainage hole with a piece of mesh, landscape cloth, or pieces of broken clay pots.

- In large, deep containers, make a bottom layer of styrofoam blocks or empty plastic jugs or bottles — you'll save on the amount of soil you need and it will make the container lighter.

- Dampen the soil mix, then add soil to the container to within a few inches/centimetres of the rim.

- If the container will be set against a wall, start from the back and plant the tall plants first, followed by the mid-range ones, then the smallest ones. If the pot will be standing in the open, start planting from the centre with the tallest plants and move toward the rim.

- Add more soil, patting and firming it around the roots to provide stability.

- Water well, then add more soil to fill in spots that have settled. The soil should be about a knuckle's measurement from the rim.

When planting a container, pick one that is large enough to balance the plant material. Generally, the tallest plant should be twice the height or width of the container.

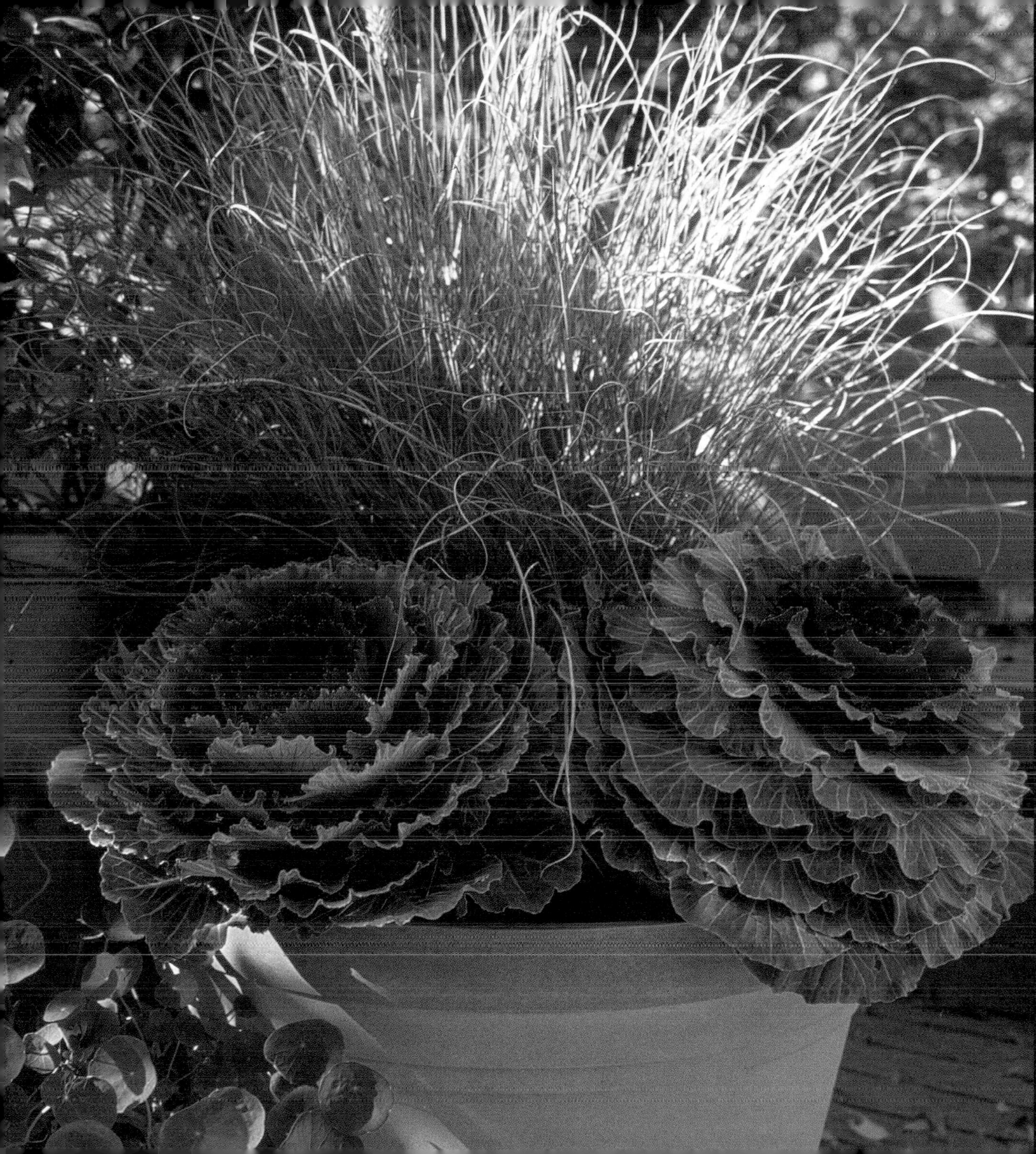

CARING FOR CONTAINER PLANTINGS

You've planted the container and it's at home on your porch or deck, gracing your front entrance or happily filling in a bare spot in the flowerbed. Now what? A little tender loving care is all that's required.

WATERING

If you do nothing else, water!

- Containers that sit in direct sunlight may need watering every day, especially in hot windy weather.
- Use a hose or watering can with a fine nozzle to avoid disturbing the soil.

A watering does double duty when used to fertilize container annuals with water-soluble plant food.

WATER WOES

It's possible to kill with kindness — container plants can be killed by overwatering. It's a dilemma. How can you give the plants the water they need but not drown them?

- Test the soil before you water — insert your finger up to the first knuckle. If the soil is wet beneath the surface, don't water.

- Be sure the container has good drainage so excess water has a way to escape. Too much water in the soil will cause the roots to rot.

- Don't let water remain in a saucer or dish under a container. Check about an hour after you've watered; discard any water that is sitting in the saucer or dish.

FERTILIZING

Vital nutrients can be washed out by watering.

- Using a slow-release fertilizer, available as plant sticks or in pellets or granules, means you don't have to worry about keeping to a schedule.

- Liquid fertilizer has the advantage of being easy to apply — just water it in about every three weeks, following the directions on the package. Never make the mixture stronger than recommended — you may damage the plants.

- Strong roots are important for container-grown plants, so choose a fertilizer high in phosphorus (one with a higher middle number).

DEADHEADING

- Nip off spent flower heads to encourage more flower and leaf production.

- Clip off dead or damaged leaves — plants in containers often come under intense scrutiny, so keep them looking top-notch.

CONTAINER CARE ON DECKS

Set saucers under pots to catch drained water and protect the surface of the deck the pot is sitting on but watch that water doesn't sit in saucers for long periods of time.

Raise containers off the deck so drained water does not collect underneath the container and promote rot.

Three small, wedge-shaped, plastic feet raise this pot of salmon-pink zonal geraniums and trailing scaevola off the wooden deck, protecting it from rot caused by water draining from the pot bottom.

PRESCRIPTIONS FOR PROBLEMS

ANIMALS

Squirrels and raccoons seem to think there's hidden treasure in those pots. There is, of course — your plants!

- Planting intensively can make it harder for those little paws to get into the soil.

- A firmly attached mesh cover, although not attractive, will protect seedlings. You can leave it in place, especially if you've planted rambunctious trailing plants that will soon grow through and over the mesh.

- Some gardeners find that a dusting of blood meal keeps squirrels away but many other gardeners have squirrels who don't realize they're not supposed to like it!

MIDSUMMER BLUES

What happened to that colourful, healthy collection of plants? Sometimes they're looking pretty sad by the middle of the summer, especially if it's been a hot and dry season.

- Maybe you haven't been deadheading enough. Get tough and shear off spent flowers and even some foliage. Lobelia and petunias can lose their oomph but will respond to a severe shearing. You might want to keep these containers in a sheltered spot for a few days after rigorous pruning.

- Don't be afraid to tear out the plants that aren't performing any more and replace them. See some suggestions on pages 54 to 61 for ideas on creating four-season containers.

Blue lobelia, right, with yellow tuberous begonias, loves cool shade and often becomes leggy in mid-summer heat, producing fewer flowers. Replace it with fresh lobelia or shear it back and feed it with half-strength liquid fertilizer to encourage more blooms.

OFF THE GROUND GARDENING

Containers are perfect for the gardener who has limited gardening space. If you're gardening off the ground — on a deck, balcony, or rooftop — there are some special considerations: the three Ws.

- Weight: Normal soil is heavy — 30 square centimetres (a cubic foot) weighs from 23 to 40 kg (50 to 90 pounds). That's why we recommend you use a lightweight soil-free planter mix. In addition, there are some tricks to controlling the weight of containers (see facing page).

- Watering: Container plants dry out more quickly than plants grown in the ground. In full sun, daily watering may become a necessity.

- Wind: The higher you go, the windier it will be. Wind hurts plants — it dries them out, damages their leaves and stems, and can even knock them over. See page 26 for some ideas about coping with wind.

SOIL TIP

Most container soil should be replaced every year, since the nutrients will be depleted. If your mixture has a lot of vermiculite or perlite, which don't contain nutrients, an annual replacement isn't necessary since you aren't relying on the soil mix to provide most of the nutrients.

An off the ground garden can be a peaceful spot to relax.

*Containers can bring colour and life to an
otherwise empty corner of a balcony.*

LIGHTEN UP!

Soil is as important in containers as it is in the ground — especially when you're gardening above ground level.

- Use a lightweight potting soil — look for one that has a lot of vermiculite or perlite in it. If you can't find one, buy your own vermiculite or perlite and add it to the mix you've bought. Up to a third of the volume of the soil can be vermiculite or perlite. Frequent fertilizing will be necessary if you use a lot of perlite or vermiculite.

- Buy lightweight containers. Good-quality plastic containers look just like terra cotta, without the heaviness of clay.

- If you have deep pots, fill the bottom with chunks of styrofoam. Or set discarded plastic pots upside down on the bottom. Many plants won't send their roots to the bottom of the pot so why fill up the unneeded space with soil?

QUENCHING CONTAINERS' THIRST

Plants dry out quickly in containers, especially when exposed to wind and intense sun, common conditions in high-rise buildings.

- Set your containers in deep saucers to catch drips but be careful that pots don't sit in saucers full of water during extended spells of rainy weather.

- Install a trickle irrigation system, available in do-it-yourself kits. They release water efficiently in a slow and continuous drip.

- Make your own wick-watering system. Insert a fabric or fibreglass wick into the soil then thread it through the bottom of the container into a water reservoir — a basin, jug, or jar. The water will travel up the wick into the soil as the soil dries out. To get the wick working, give the container a good initial watering; after that, just keep the jug topped up.

- Buy a container that employs a bottom-watering system. The newest feature "soil-sipping" columns that wick water up naturally from a bottom reservoir.

Right: Moss-lined hanging baskets, such as this gorgeous one planted with pink impatiens, silver dusty Miller, geraniums, fuchsias, lobelia, and nemesia, require frequent watering — sometimes twice daily in hot, windy weather.

BLOWING IN THE WIND

These ideas for protecting your plants have a bonus: they'll protect you too!

- Install screens or awnings to protect your plants. Choose wind-permeable screens — rigid solid structures will cause turbulence as the winds come into contact with them.

- Trellises can double as screens — the plants you grow up them may suffer somewhat but they will protect the other plants.

Blue-stained lattice acts as a privacy screen for this charming sundeck while providing wind protection for the container plants.

CHOOSING PLANTS FOR CONTAINER DESIGN

You've probably got the idea we think design is important — and we do! In our book *Plantings*, we talk about the layers of a garden, from the canopy of tall trees to the creeping ground cover. The same concept applies to planting containers — think of them as landscapes in miniature. When you design your container, think of the hierarchy of height — those wonderful, tumbling trailers, the mid-range plants and the tall plants.

Each type of plant fulfills a particular function in the design.

- The trailing plants soften the composition, hiding the edges of the container, and sometimes even obscuring the entire container.

- The mid-range plants, which might be bushy or spreading, provide bulk, or filler, and an opportunity to showcase favourite plants.

- The tall, upright plants give height.

Another aspect of design is in the individual plants themselves — the shape and texture of their leaves, the shape and colour of their flowers, the type of stem, the overall shape of the plant. Combine and contrast textures, shapes, and colours to create the type of container that suits your setting, whether you have a formal or informal garden.

COLOUR

Containers give you a great chance to play with colour, to test what works and what doesn't. What are the effects of different colours?

- Coolness: conveyed by blue, lavender, green, blue-green, grey

- Warmth: conveyed by red, yellow, orange

- Serenity: an all-green scheme, dependent on foliage and texture, is restful; good for shady areas

- Evening: containers filled with white-flowered plants, or plants with variegated foliage, will be more visible at night

A Muskoka chair and side-table have been painted candy-pink to pick up the colour theme of this sundeck garden. The pots are planted with pink cascading geraniums, 'Pink Wave' petunias and trailing purple scaevola.

TRAILING PLANTS

Use trailing plants to
- soften the edges of containers
- hide the pot portion of containers

Check out the section on Annual Vines, page 38. Many of these plants don't have to grow up — let them drape themselves over the edges of the container.

SOME GREAT TRAILERS

Flowering Plants

> ### PLANTING TIP
>
> Given their single-season life spans, annuals work well as container plants. Some adventuresome gardeners like to grow perennials or clematis in containers as well. (These plants are covered on pages 40 to 42.)

SWAN RIVER DAISY (*Brachycome iberidifolia*): White or medium-blue daisy-like flowers with yellow or dark centres; doesn't mind being cramped; blooms best in full sun; its finely divided leaves soften container edges

LOBELIA (*Lobelia*): Trailing type has masses of delicate flowers in blue, purple, or white; shade or part sun; may falter in summer heat and humidity — try shearing it back to renew

SCAEVOLA (*Scaevola aemula*): Purple flowers smother this plant throughout the summer; let dry out between watering but don't neglect it; sun; simply one of the best trailers for sunny containers

MOSS ROSE (*Portulaca*): Pretty flowers with delicate-looking blooms in white, yellow, red, peach; fleshy needle-like foliage; tolerates drought; buds close in cloudy weather; sandy soil and full sun

BIDENS (*Bidens ferulifolia*): Vigorous trailer with small yellow daisy-like flowers on long, clambering, stiff stems; heat tolerant; full sun

This spectacular railing planter contains a colourful variety of trailing plants including, from left, white nierembergia, purple scaevola, velvety silver-grey licorice plant (Helichrysum petiolare) *and pink cascading geraniums. At the top are orange and yellow tuberous begonias and ageratum 'Blue Horizon'.*

DAHLBERG DAISY (*Dyssodia tenuiloba*): Low-growing with tiny yellow flowers and ferny, pungent leaves; drought-tolerant; full sun

CALIBRACOA 'MILLION BELLS': New petunia-like species developed commercially in Japan; heavy-blooming; purple, pink, or white flowers; full sun

CONVOLVULUS (*Convolvulus sabatius*): Slender trailing stems to 45 cm (18 inches) with blue, morning glory-like flowers; full sun; best in warm weather

IVY-LEAF GERANIUM (*Pelargonium peltatum*): Lots of flowers throughout the summer in shades of pink, lilac, salmon, scarlet; leaves are similar to ivy; look for floriferous 'Balcon' geraniums, too; especially wonderful in hanging baskets; sun

PETUNIA (*Petunia*): Cascading petunias are useful for their wide range of cheerful colours — white, blue, pink, yellow, violet, scarlet; keep it deadheaded for good flower production — don't be afraid to pinch back quite hard to make it become nice and bushy; sun; 'Purple Wave' and 'Pink Wave' produce a colourful 120-cm (4-foot) carpet of flowers

BACOPA (*Sutera cordata*): Tiny white flowers along stiff stems covered with small rounded leaves; tolerates dryness; sun; provides good texture; for a change, try the mauve or pink varieties

VERBENA (*Verbena*): Wide choice of growth habits and colour combinations — red, purple, pink, blue; full sun; our favourites are 'Tapien Purple' and 'Tapien Pink'

NIEREMBERGIA (*Nierembergia*): Spreads in a neat mound shape; flowers of 'Purple Robe' is blue to violet with a golden centre, 'Mont Blanc' is a white variety — all make good additions to a colour scheme of blue, silver, and white; full sun; flowers are a pretty cup shape, hence its common name of cup flower

A lovely colour combination for a window box or balcony planter: trailing burgundy-wine petunias, yellow calceolaria, lavender, campanula and blue marguerite or kingfisher daisy (Felicia amelloides)

Foliage Plants

HELICHRYSUM (*Helichrysum petiolare*): Also called the licorice plant; it's used for its furry grey foliage; stiff low arching stems help support floppier plants; sun or partial shade; one of our all-time favourites, especially 'Icicles', which looks like tiny delicate icicles — use it with bacopa for a stunning combination

VARIEGATED MINT LEAF (*Plectranthus madagascariensis*): Excellent foliage trailer with scented frilly, white-edged scented leaves on long branching stems; part shade; looks great with silver, blue, and yellow combinations

IVIES (*Hedera*): Choose for their various shades of green and different textures; shade and part sun

ASPARAGUS FERN (*Asparagus plumosus*): Used for its soft needle-like foliage held on long arching stems; shade or sun

MID-RANGE PLANTS

Use these plants
- for filling the middle
- as background for trailers

SOME GREAT MID-RANGE PLANTS

Flowering Plants

IMPATIENS (*Impatiens*): Masses of white, pink, or red flowers in single colours or stunning combinations of two or three colours; water frequently in hot windy weather; shade; in our view, they can't be overused; New Guinea impatiens can be used in full sun or part shade — plants are upright or spreading, with large, sometimes variegated leaves and flowers in lavender, purple, pink, orange, or red

DIANTHUS (*Dianthus*): Spiky grey-green foliage and white, pink, or red blooms; full sun; spicy fragrance; foliage works well with many colour schemes; use the red to add zing to more restrained combinations

GERANIUM (*Geranium*): Often used on its own, but makes good addition to cottagey plantings; white, red, pink; sun

NASTURTIUM (*Nasturium*): Varieties are mounded or trailing; heat-resistant; cream, yellow, orange; sun; pair with a trailer such as a creamy white verbena or petunia — nice on its own or at the foot of a standard yellow hibiscus

PERSIAN VIOLET (*Exacum affine*): Mounded and trailing varieties available; violet-blue blooms; shade

BROWALLIA (*Browallia*): Nice mid-range sprawler; blue, deep blue, or white flowers for those silver-blue-white combinations; shade-tolerant

FUCHSIA (*Fuchsia*): On its own or in combination (*careful* combination — its colours are not always easy to match with others); red, pink, or purple flowers hang from cascading branches; shade; makes great candidate for training as a standard

ROSES

Not enough space to grow roses? Go crazy with miniatures and patio roses! Even in large gardens, there's a spot for a container full of these diminutive lovelies. Put them in a row marching up the front steps, as a centrepiece on an outdoor table, or as part of a mixed planting in a large container.

Bonus — miniatures overwinter! Remove them from their pots in autumn and plant them, well-mulched, in the garden.

BLUE MARGUERITE (*Felicia*): Periwinkle blue petals around a yellow centre; full sun; part trailer, part mid-range, makes a stunning display on its own

MARGUERITE DAISY (*Chrysanthemum frutescens*): Shrubby plant with yellow or white daisy-like flowers; blooms profusely all summer; full sun; looks lovely on its own or with some trailers gracing the edges of the container

NICOTINE (*Nicotiana alata*): Height varies according to variety — 'Domino' series grows to a maximum of 36 cm (14 inches) and has a bushy form that produces lots of flowers; 'Nicki', which also has lots of flowers in a wide range of colours, grows to 46 cm (18 inches); full sun to full shade

SALVIA (*Salvia*): Blue salvia (*S. farinacea*) works well with combinations of silver and yellow; use red (*S. splendens*) with care — adds zing to an otherwise lifeless combination; both bloom all summer; sun

Foliage Plants

COLEUS (*Coleus*): Popular because of its variegated foliage; leaves are green (including lime green), red, or deep burgundy; shade; the lime can be hard to place sometimes — use on its own or combine with silver and white plants, with a dash of burgundy

DUSTY MILLER (*Senecio cineraria*): Another foliage plant; silvery lacy foliage; heat-resistant; sun; tone down hot colours with this plant

Raspberry-pink geraniums and purple browallia make a stunning duo in filtered sunlight.

PLANTS FOR HEIGHT

Use these plants for
- anchoring the design
- providing a backdrop for the lower-growing plants
- adding drama to a composition
- balancing the size of the container

SOME GREAT TALL PLANTS

Flowering Plants

LANTANA (*Lantana*): Stiff coarse plant; white, yellow, orange, pink, purple, red lavender; prune at beginning and middle of season; sun; makes wonderful standard

ROSE MALLOW (*Lavatera trimestris*): Similar to a hollyhock, with white or pink silky flowers; sun; prefers cool weather and low humidity

CHINA ASTER (*Callistephus chinesis*): Large white, pink, purple, or red chrysanthemum-type flowers; may need staking or team with plants that can prop it up; full sun; use in late summer/fall containers

STANDARD CENTREPIECES

Container plants trained as standards — plants that grow from strong central stems — make elegant focal points or add a touch of formality when used in pairs. Some plants that make impressive standards are lantana, heliotrope, hibiscus, mandevilla, marguerites, fuchsia, and rosemary.

To make your own standard, choose a plant with a strong straight stem. Remove branches from the bottom two-thirds of the stem as the plant grows.

Provide support for the young stem by inserting a stake in the container and attaching the stem to the stake with twist ties or something more decorative, such as raffia. It may take more than one season for your plant to reach its desired height.

If the do-it-yourself method is too slow, buy plants that have already been trained as standards and add a frothy underplanting of one of the trailers we described on pages 30 to 33.

GRASSES FOR CONTAINERS

Use grasses alone as a bold statement or to add interest to other plantings in a large container. If you grow them singly, set the container among other containers for a stunning display.

COSMOS (*Cosmos*): Graceful with ferny foliage and flower colours ranging from white and orange through pink to magenta; sun; available in a variety of heights; provides nice texture

MOTHER GERANIUM (*Pelargonium*): Profuse, multi-stemmed plants that give a full lush look — get the 10-inch pots for maximum effect;sun; great flowers

CAPE MALLOW (*Anisodontea capensis*): Tender shrub sold as annual; masses of small coral flowers on stiff branches; pinch shoots to encourage bushiness; full sun

Foliage Plants

BLACK MONDO GRASS (*Ophiopogon 'Nigrescens'*): Striking purple-black foliage; lovely contrast plant; sun or shade

BLUE FESCUES (*Festuca*): small grasses for sunny containers; perennial

> Spiky foliage accents for centre of containers include dracaena, cordylines, and New Zealand flax

DRACENA (*Dracaena*): Narrow, sword-shaped leaves provide contrast to trailing or compact plants; sun or partial shade

LEMON GRASS (*Cymbopogon citratus*): Gives off a strong scent of lemon; blades, which grow quite tall, are about 2.5 cm (1 inch) wide

PAPYRUS (*Cyperus*): Graceful, tall, dark green stems; needs wet rich soil; grows quickly and needs to be protected from strong winds; keep indoors over winter as house plant; sun or shade

BLUE OAT GRASS (*Helictotrichon*): Low-growing, rounded plant; makes a nice contrast to taller grasses; full sun but not keen on hot humid summers; perennial

ANNUAL VINES

We can't imagine container growing without vines — they're great in small spaces such as balconies, where they take up little floor space. Use them

- as a temporary screen to hide a view
- to cover a post
- to provide some shade.

SOME GREAT ANNUAL VINES

BLACK-EYED SUSAN VINE (*Thunbergia alata*): Quick-growing twining climber; also spills down; useful at the edge of a container or scrambling up a small trellis; leaves shaped like arrowheads and soft yellow, white, or orange daisy-like flowers; sun, part shade

MORNING GLORIES (*Ipomoea*): Twining climber; range of colours: white, fabulous blues, reds; sun

CUP AND SAUCER VINE (*Cobaea scandens*): Not surprisingly, the flowers are cup- or bell-shaped; purple, lavender, or white; vigorous grower; full sun

CHILEAN GLORY VINE (*Eccremocarpus scaber*): Masses of tiny red or yellow flowers; full sun

HYACINTH BEAN (*Dolichos lablab*): Purplish green leaves and purple or white sweet pea-like flowers; full sun

PURPLE BELL VINE (*Rhodochiton atrosanguineum*): Delicate reddish-purple flowers; good on wire circle or bent bamboo trellis in small pot

SWEET PEA (*Lathyrus odoratus*): Wonderful variety of colours, not all of which are scented; full sun, but not extreme heat unless marked heat resistant, or some shade

POTATO VINE (*Solanum jasminoides*): A twiner with purple-tinged leaves and clusters of white or purple flowers; prefers afternoon shade

Pink and white morning glories are lovely paired with blue plumbago.

DESIGN TIP

An annual vine with a vertical support, such as an obelisk, adds height to a container and the garden. One of these non-stop bloomers with a trailing plant at its feet is a complete, and satisying, composition.

*Purple bell vine (Rhodochiton),
trained on curved bamboo stakes
inserted into a pot, forms a pretty
bower over orchid-pink petunias
and trailing verbena.*

PERENNIALS

I f you're a risk-taking gardener, growing perennials in containers will give you a challenge. It can be done, especially if you live in Zone 6 or milder (see our book *Care* for information about zones).

THE CHALLENGE

In a word, the challenge is winter — or rather, freezing. The roots of container-grown plants are more exposed to temperature fluctuations than those of plants grown in the ground. On a hot day, the roots will heat up more quickly, especially if the container is a dark colour, and on a cold day, they will freeze more quickly. But even more damaging than these extremes is the constant change between freezing and thawing, as well as the effects of drying winter winds.

Here are some tips to ensure your perennials have a chance of surviving. The most important thing is to protect each plant's root ball.

- Use as big a container as possible.
- Line a square or rectangular container with sheets of styrofoam cut to fit snugly inside the container.
- In a round container, use foam nuggets (the kind used in packing) — but they won't provide as much protection as rigid styrofoam.
- In addition, set the container inside another container and fill the space between the two with insulation.
- As winter approaches, protect the container further by mounding bags of leaves around it. If possible, move it to a sheltered spot where it will be protected from drying winds and snow and rain which can exert a deadly freeze-thaw effect on the plants' crown.
- The entire container can be buried in the garden for the winter, although obviously this depends on the size and weight of the plant and container.
- Protect container evergreens by watering them well right up until the soil has frozen, then swaddle them in burlap to protect from drying winds. Spraying them with anti-desiccants will also protect them.
- Container shrubs and small trees can be pruned and stored in protected sheds or garages.

SOME PERENNIALS TO TRY

Perennials don't have as long a blooming period as most annuals but that doesn't mean you can't find some that will produce blooms for a satisfying length of time. So look for perennials with attractive or interesting foliage or shape. You can also mix in some of our favourite trailers from pages 30 to 33.

Here are some good candidates for growing in containers — we don't guarantee they'll survive a winter, but if they do, they'll grow quickly!

HOSTA (*Hosta*): Perfect for the shady garden; grow them for their lovely foliage

DAYLILY (*Hemerocallis*): Depending on variety, blooms early in the season — look for 'Stella de Oro' for a long blooming period; available in wide range of colours; graceful foliage; sun

LAVENDER (*Lavandula*): Shrubby and fragrant with needlike grey foliage and delicate lavender flowers; may actually survive longer in a container given the care described than in the garden; sun

BELLFLOWER (*Campanula*): Some are perennial, some annual, some are tall, some are short, some trail, others are upright; taller varieties might need staking; colours are blue, lavender, purple, white, or pink; sun or partial shade

LILY (*Lilium*): Short blooming time, but spectacular when flowering — each bloom is large and some are highly fragrant; by choosing varieties that flower at different times in the summer, you can have a continuous display; sun, regular deep watering in hot weather; keep roots cool by underplanting with sweet alyssum or another trailer

With its felted silvery leaves, perennial lambs' ears (Stachys lanata) *make an unusual edging plant in this large half-barrel.*

CONTAINER CLEMATIS

*A handsome wooden obelisk supports
a container-grown clematis.*

Certain large-flowered Group 2 clematis with a compact growth habit are best for containers. (See our book *Care* for more information on clematis groups). Ultra-hardy (Zone 2-3) C. *macropetala* hybrids stand a good chance of surviving winter in a large container, but flower only in spring.

HOW TO PLANT

1. In the bottom of a large container, put a layer at least 5 cm (2 inches) of pebbles or broken pottery. Raise the container off the ground with bricks so that drainage holes are not blocked.

2. Use PC Better Than Topsoil or another top-quality potting soil to fill the container. Each spring replace the top 6 to 8 cm (2 to 3 inches) of soil with fresh potting soil.

3. Plant the clematis, burying the root crown 6 to 8 cm (2 to 3 inches) below the surface of the soil in the container. Plant some trailers around the clematis to provide shade and shelter for the roots.

4. Insert or provide a support for the clematis, or let it spill over the edges of the container. If you provide a support, keep in mind that to give the clematis the best chance of survival, you will need to move the container to a protected spot over the winter but will not want to remove the season's growth. The protected spot should be out of snow and rain to prevent winter's freeze/thaw cycle from damaging the clematis crown.

5. When you first bring the container out in the spring, cut back the previous year's growth to 24 cm (9 inches) to encourage new stems. Cut back to a pair of buds. When three pairs of leaves have formed, remove the growing tip so that more stems will be produced from each stem. This first-year pruning effectively removes flower buds, since Group 2 clematis flower only on old growth, but is necessary to develop a well-branched vine. In the second and subsequent years, only light spring pruning of Group 2 clematis is required to tidy the vine and restrict its height.

6. Train new growth, tying if necessary, to cover the support.

7. Water well, daily if weather is dry.

8. Fertilize with PC Clematis and Vine Food in early spring and early summer.

RECOMMENDED FOR CONTAINERS

- 'Arctic Queen' • 'Beth Currie' • 'Guernsey Cream' • 'Royal Velvet'
- 'Edouard Desfosse' • 'Multi-Blue' • 'Scartho Gem'

TREES IN CONTAINERS

Y ou don't have to have an Italian villa to grow larger specimens in containers. Naturally, these potted plants will face the same problems as perennials — the stress of alternate freezing and thawing during winter. And because they're larger, they're likely to be in a permanent setting, particularly on rooftops or decks.

Nevertheless, it is possible to succeed by using large, well-insulated containers or planting boxes and selecting dwarf varieties of the hardiest plants available — usually those native to areas several zones colder than your own.

In many cases, periodic bonsai-style root pruning with corresponding reduction of the above-ground growth will keep plants at an appropriate size for their containers.

SMALL DECIDUOUS TREES:

Amur chokecherry (*Prunus maackii*) — Zone 2b
Amur maple (*Acer ginnala*) — Zone 1b
Chokecherry (*Prunus virginiana*) — Zone 2
Siberian crabapple (*Malus baccata*) — Zone 2b
Pagoda dogwood (*Cornus alternifolia*) — Zone 3b
Mountain ash (*Sorbus*) — Zone 3

SLOW-GROWING OR SMALL CONIFERS:

Bristlecone pine (*Pinus aristata*) — Zone 3
Dwarf Scots pine (*Pinus sylvestris* 'Watereri') — Zone 2
Mugo pine (*Pinus mugo*) — Zone 2b
Ohlendorffi Norway spruce (*Picea abies* 'Ohlendorffi') — Zone 3
Dwarf Alberta spruce (*Picea glauca* 'Conica') — Zone 2
Dwarf Colorado blue spruce (*Picea pungens* 'Glauca Globosa') — Zone 2
White cedar or arborvitae (*Thuja occidentalis*) — Zone 2b
Juniper, common (*Juniperus communis*) — Zone 4
Japanese yew (*Taxus cuspidata*) — Zone 4

BROADLEAF EVERGREENS:

It is essential to protect these plants from wind and afternoon sun.

Rhododendron 'PJM' and related Mezitt cultivars — Zone 3-4
Rhododendron 'Northern Lights' series — Zone 3-4
Korean boxwood — Zone 5

DECIDUOUS SHRUBS:

Siberian peashrub (*Caragana arborescens*) — Zone 2
Tatarian dogwood (*Cornus alba*) — Zone 2
Russian olive (*Eleagnus angustifolius*) — Zone 2
Burning bush (*Euonymus alatus*) — Zone 3
Smooth hydrangea (*Hydrangea arborescens*) — Zone 2b
Mock orange (*Philadelphus*) — some Zone 3
Ninebark (*Physocarpus*) — Zone 2b
Potentilla (*Potentilla fruticosa*) — Zone 2
Nanking cherry (*Prunus tomentosa*) — Zone 2
Flowering almond (*Prunus triloba*) — Zone 2b
Alpine currant (*Ribes alpinum*) — Zone 2
Rugosa rose (*Rosa rugosa*) — Zone 2
Spireas, various (*Spiraea*) — Zone 2-3

DWARF APPLES

Imagine your own apple tree on your back deck. Not all dwarf apples are considered winter-hardy so check carefully and note whether they're self-pollinating — they should be. When preparing the tree for the winter, protect the top as well as the roots.

COLONNADE APPLES

Try a four-in-one fruit tree — each tree bears four different varieties. Choose an apple, pear, or cherry — or one of each. The Colonnade apple tree won't grow more than 2.5 m (8 feet). It has a single trunk, and the apples are borne on short fruiting spurs that project from the trunk.

SPECIAL CONTAINERS: A POND IN A POT

Goldfish, waterlilies, and splashing fountains aren't just for gardeners with big backyards. Watertight containers let you bring the magic of water gardening to your balcony, deck, or rooftop.

Glazed pots and bowls are sophisticated additions to a patio, a deck, or garden, and can look lovely planted with a miniature waterlily cultivar such as orange 'Graziella', yellow 'Pygmaea Helvola' or blue 'Dauben'.

A half-barrel lined with flexible PVC or EPDM pond-liner, or with its own rigid fibreglass shell, makes a rustic container lily pond, and will hold several aquatic plants and a few goldfish. Introduce goldfish the way you would in a large water garden — lower the bag they're in into the pot and let the temperature of the water in the container and the bag equalize before releasing them. In addition, you'll need to add fresh water not only to top up water lost by evaporation but to supply constant fresh water for the fish. Let tapwater sit overnight before adding to the water garden or use a dechlorinating agent, available where golfish are sold.

WINTER CARE: Container water gardens need to be emptied in autumn to prevent freezing and breakage in winter. Store hardy aquatic plants in a cool place or treat them as annuals. Move goldfish to a cold water aquarium indoors.

Marginal aquatics such as dwarf bulrush and dwarf papyrus, left, make interesting plants for container water gardens.

*There are many dwarf water lily cultivars that are
perfectly suited for container water gardens.*

SPECIAL CONTAINER GARDENS: SUCCULENTS AND ALPINES

SUCCULENTS

The easiest plants to look after are those that need little watering, little fertilizing, and no deadheading. Succulents fill the bill. As well, they're attractive — not so much for their flowers as for their fleshy leaves. When you see fleshy leaves on a plant, you can make an assumption: the plant can tolerate fairly lengthy periods without water. This ability to survive a bit of benign neglect makes them ideal for using at summer cottages, weekend homes, and hot dry areas.

Another advantage to using succulents is that they can survive in small containers. This gives you lots of flexibility to move the containers around for different effects. By putting one specimen in its own container, you draw attention to that particular plant. Finally, because many succulents need to be wintered indoors, they're easier to bring inside when grown in small containers. Finally, because many succulents need to be wintered indoors, they're easier to bring inside when grown in small containers.

Many succulents are a little odd looking but they have wonderful shapes and subtle colours. Here are some to watch for.

Above, *A cactus in a distinctive container thrives in the sun and heat of a rooftop garden.* Right, *A heat-loving succulent dish garden features blue-grey echeveria, dragon's blood sedum and creeping orange* Portulaca pilosa.

HENS AND CHICKS (*Echeveria imbricata*)
DONKEY'S TAIL (*Sedum morganianum*)
MOTHER-IN-LAW'S TONGUE (*Sansevieria trifasciata*)
JADE TREE (*Crassula argentea*)
MOONSTONES (*Pachyphytum oviferum*)
HOUSELEEK (*Sempervivum*)
CACTUS, many varieties

ALPINES

Many alpine plants flower only in the spring but they also have attractive foliage and shapes — tufts, mats, rosettes, trailers, and cushions. Because alpine plants tend to be small, they can get lost in large containers and when combined with other plants. But displayed in dish gardens — attractive hand-thrown pots, sinks, or faux-stone troughs — they dress up a table, deck, or entryway from spring to fall.

Here are some plants that look great in dish gardens — you'll find them at your favourite gardening shop.

SAXIFRAGE (*Saxifraga*)
PINKS (*Dianthus*)
THRIFT (*Armeria*)
MOSS PHLOX (*Phlox subulata*)
ALYSSUM (*Alyssum*)
ROCK ROSE (*Helianthemum nummularium*)
STONECROP (*Sedum*)
HOUSELEEK (*Sempervivum*)

SOIL TIP

Make sure containers for alpines are well drained and the soil is gritty rather than rich. A mulch of fine pebbles or gravel makes them picture-perfect.

SPECIAL CONTAINER GARDENS: VEGETABLES

This summer, grow your own vegetables in containers and enjoy delights such as freshly picked tomatoes, lettuce, and carrots — yes, even carrots! Many miniature vegetable varieties have been bred especially for growing in containers. Look for dwarf vegetables in seed catalogues.

Tomatoes are a great choice for container growing, if they're kept well watered and fertilized.

LETTUCE

One of the easiest vegetables to grow in a container, lettuce does best in cool weather and has the advantage of growing well in partial shade. Although it looks attractive on its own, mix lettuce with flowers for a fun combination.

SPINACH

Another easy cool-weather vegetable, spinach can give you two crops — one in early summer, the other in early fall. And its dark green leaves make a nice contrast to the lighter lettuce leaves.

RADISHES

Fast and easy to grow, radishes need lots of water to make them crisp and tender. You'll get a crop within three or four weeks of planting. Once hot weather arrives, they'll languish so get them started early in the spring. As you pull a radish, plant another seed to keep a steady supply.

PEAS

Almost nothing can match a meal of freshly picked peas — except perhaps tomatoes. Start the seeds early and provide them with a trellis, chicken wire, or nylon mesh to scramble up.

BEANS

Beans like warm weather so sow late in the spring in a large container. Once the beans have formed, keep picking them to encourage more production. Bush beans need no support; pole runner beans need stakes. Both types need full sun.

CARROTS

Containers provide ideal conditions for carrots — you'll get strong, straight, crunchy results. When you buy the seed, check the mature length to be sure you're providing enough depth for the crop. Look for names such as 'Tiny Sweet', 'Little Finger', and 'Gold Nugget'. Thin your seedlings as they grow.

TOMATOES

If you try nothing else, grow your own tomatoes! Even the most crowded deck or porch can accommodate a small pot of cherry tomatoes. Tomatoes of all sizes love hot weather and lots of sun but don't let them get scorched. Protect them from wind as much as possible. Keep them well watered for plump, juicy fruit and use a fertilizer formulated for tomatoes. If you grow vine-type or indeterminate tomatoes, stake them early so you don't damage the roots later.

"MESCLUN" SALAD MIX

You've seen those lovely mixes of gourmet salad greens in the supermarket — but did you know how easy it is to grow your own? Look for the following seeds and sow them together in one container. Mesclun is a "cut-and-come-again" crop, so as the seedlings grow, start to harvest them and new ones will take their place.

Arugula
Beets (harvest the young leaves)
Corn salad
Cress
Leaf lettuce, red and green
Spinach
Endive
Mustard
Chives

SPECIAL CONTAINER GARDENS: HERBS

Probably the most popular edible plants to grow in containers are herbs. They add flavour to foods such as soups, salads, stews, and sandwich fillings. On their own, some herbs may not be especially great to look at, but planting a combination of herbs together can give you a "miniature landscape in a pot." If herbs are grown individually, cluster the containers in groups for a pretty presentation.

Herbs grow best in well-drained humus-rich soil. Most of them are sun-lovers and can withstand some drought.

BASIL

- Several varieties, in green and purple; some have large leaves (the best ones for pesto), some have small leaves; grow both kinds for contrast; annual

CHIVES

- Onion-flavoured or garlic-flavoured, depending on variety; perennial
- Fluffy, ball-shaped purple or pink flowers cluster at the end of long thin leaves

DILL

- Grows fairly tall with a flat head; airy yellow flowers and feathery foliage; annual; dwarf variety 'Fernleaf' is good for growing in pots

MARJORAM

- Two kinds: pot has long stems; sweet has grey leaves; annual

HERBS AND FLOWERS

We like to see flowers and herbs growing together — they make pretty companions. Here are a few ideas:

- Plant dill with lower-growing annuals. Its feathery foliage and attractive heads make a nice lacy texture.

- Scatter small pots of herbs around larger containers of flowering plants for an easy-to-change "landscape."

- Use creeping thyme or oregano instead of bacopa to soften the edge of a container or hanging basket.

- Rosemary and oregano or thyme make perfect companions in containers as well as on the dinner table.

MINT

- Perfect for containers, invasive in the garden; perennial

OREGANO

- Sprawler with small leaves — if used with other plants in a container, plant near the edges; annual

PARSLEY

- Two main varieties: one has curly leaves;, the other, Italian parsley, has flat leaves; biannual
- A "mid-range" plant when in a combined container planting

ROSEMARY

- Needle-like grey foliage
- Bring indoors in the winter — it just might survive!

SAGE

- Grey leaves with a slightly puckered texture; look for attractive gold-variegated and purple varieties
- Short-lived perennial

COMMON THYME (*Thymus vulgaris*)

- is bushy; its aromatic leaves are used in cooking; has grey-green leaves and white or pale lavender blossoms; lemon thyme (*T. x citriodorus*) has strong lemon scent; dark green leaves and white flowers; mother-of-thyme (*T. serpyllum*) is a creeping plant and has small, dark green leaves and pink to purple flowers.

When grown in a container, basil can be treated to the rich soil and warmth it requires to thrive.

THE FOUR SEASONS OF A CONTAINER

Our climate isn't kind to keen gardeners — most of us contend with our gardens hiding under great drifts of snow for several months a year. Others deal with days of rain that saturates the soil, keeping us indoors as surely as a blizzard would. But does that mean we should give up on containers? Absolutely not.

Your four-season containers can grace your balcony, your deck, your front porch — just make sure you pick a container that can withstand the ravages of winter.

In the spring, summer, and fall, you can use terra cotta or ceramic containers. But winter is different. Choose your winter container carefully. Sturdy plastic, wood, cement, or cast iron are all good candidates. And although you won't be growing plants in them in the winter, you'll need some soil to anchor the creative arrangements of branches, dried reeds and grasses, and ornaments you make.

In the next few pages, we'll give you some ideas for spring, summer, fall, and winter containers.

On a shady front porch, a romantic look is achieved with foliage plants including trailing variegated mint-leaf (Plectranthus madagascariensis), *heuchera 'Palace Purple' and a hydrangea that started out blue, but aged to green in the shade. The finishing touch is a pussy-willow bow.*

THE SPRING CONTAINER

In nearly all parts of the country, March and April aren't too early to start a spring container. That's when stores set out pots of pansies, quickly followed by flowering bulbs and primroses.

PLANTING WITHOUT SOIL

If you've got some potting soil tucked away in the house, you can use it. But if not, don't worry. You don't really need it.

- Choose a fairly shallow container.
- Buy some sheet moss or Spanish moss.
- Line the container with the moss.
- Leave the plants in their pots and nestle the pots in the moss.
- Once you've arranged the plants to your satisfaction, tease some of the moss up around the pots to hide their rims.

THE PLANTS

- Pansies and violas are quite frost-tolerant. The textures of these closely related plants complement each other well.
- Primroses — for many people, the first sign of spring.
- Grape hyacinth — team them with primroses for a stunning display.
- Tulips and daffodils give height and added colour; their long narrow leaves contrast with rounder pansy or primrose foliage.
- Don't overlook smaller bulbs such as snowdrops, crocus, iris reticulata.
- When bulbs have finished blooming, remove them from their pots with their foliage intact. Leave them to dry in a protected spot and plant them in the garden in the fall.
- Plant primroses in the garden when they have finished flowering.

Pansies, in spite of their delicate faces, can be set out early in the season and enjoyed in containers of all shapes and sizes.

THE SUMMER CONTAINER:
BRINGING THE TROPICS TO A POT NEAR YOU

Increasingly, tropical shrubs, vines, and bulbs are being used to bring a burst of colour to summer containers. It's not surprising since these warm-weather lovers originate in countries with year-round climates similar to our summers.

You can overwinter them by bringing them indoors in late summer and treating them as tender houseplants.

Here are some tropicals to introduce to the outdoors in very late spring or early summer, when the weather has warmed up nicely.

ABUTILON OR FLOWERING MAPLE (*Abutilon*): Nodding single flowers in yellow, peach, red, cream or orange; some cultivars have yellow-splashed leaves; sun or light shade

BOUGAINVILLEA (*Bougainvillea*): Tropical vine for large pot or planter; needs very warm temperatures; sun

ANGEL'S TRUMPET (*Brugmansia*): Beautiful but poisonous shrub with pendulous white, yellow, orange or purple flowers; often fragrant; sun

HIBISCUS (*Hibiscus rosa-sinensis*): Popular tropical with large single or double flowers in many brilliant colors; prune back in spring for best bloom; sun

MANDEVILLA (*Mandevilla*): Both the tall, vining pink-flowered 'Alice duPont' and shrubby 'Little Red Riding Hood' make outstanding easy-care container plants; full sun

OLEANDER (*Nerium oleander*): Dark green, leathery, glossy leaves; flowers — often fragrant — are white, yellow, pink, salmon, or red; sun; needs little watering once established; all parts of the plant are poisonous

PASSIONFLOWER (*Passiflora*): Vines with wonderfully exotic-looking flowers of purple or pink; cut back annually; full sun

PLUMBAGO (*Plumbago capensis*): Easy, tall shrub (can be used as a vine) with light blue, phlox-like flowers; shear in spring; sun

STAR JASMINE (*Trachelospermum jasminoides*): Needs support; new foliage is glossy and light green, older foliage is dark and lustrous; clusters of small, intensely-fragrant, white pinwheel-like flowers; sun or light shade

Shrubby pink oleander and a red-flowered hibiscus standard enjoy a summer holiday on a patio outside the solarium where they've overwintered.

THE SUMMER CONTAINER:
TAKING HOUSEPLANTS ON VACATION

Tender container houseplants such as palms, dracaenas, Rex begonias, hibiscus, peperomias, scented geraniums, clivias, and orchids appreciate a summer vacation in the great outdoors. Just make sure night temperatures are sufficiently warm when you bring plants out, at least 15°C (60°F). Keep them out of direct sunlight for the first few days — they need time to become acclimatized to the sudden change.

In the late summer, bring them indoors before the weather turns chilly. Watch for hitchhiking pests when you bring them in. Quarantine returning vacationers from your other houseplants for several days. If insects appear, treat plant and soil with insecticidal soap spray, reapplying after four to five days if problems persist.

Left, *A raised terrace is the summer home for a large collection of conservatory plants. Two container water gardens flank the stairs.* Here, *An old-fashioned rex begonia houseplant spends summer on the porch in the outstretched "arms" of this unique container.*

THE FALL CONTAINER

Yes, you can plant just chrysanthemums — but don't stop there . . .

- Try something different — how about using a bushel basket for a container? It will look right at home with a scattering of pumpkins at its base as Hallowe'en approaches.

- We've already mentioned chrysanthemums — we love them for their rich bronzes, yellows, purples, pinks, and whites.

- Asters are delicate, with their fringed, daisy-like flowers. They come in a variety of heights, from tall to dwarf, and the colour range provides lots of choices — blue, pink, lavender, purple, white and red.

- Ornamental kale and cabbage look like lacy bouquets held inside stiff green doilies. They come in pink, purple, green, white, and combinations of these colours.

- Combine dried grasses and rushes with some branches of colourful leaves to perk up the front entrance.

- Haunt the garden centres and pick up some mature end-of-season bargains for quick, lush plantings.

A formal urn celebrates autumn and harvest time with an arrangement of Savoy cabbages, sunflower heads, annual fountain grass and a potted cutleaf sumac (Rhus typhina 'Disssectum'), just turning colour.

THE WINTER CONTAINER

Snow is coming — and if you've never attempted a winter container, you'll find it easy to be inspired.

- If you've been doing some late-season pruning of evergreens, hold on to those boughs and branches. They're the foundation for winter arrangements.

- Less is more — try simple branches displayed in an elegant container.

- Get out the spray paint. Gold, bronze, or silver enamel can put a festive touch on conifer branches; it can even extend the season for ornamental kale or sunflowers.

- Decorate natural or gilded branches with red and green bows or twine tiny lights along their lengths.

An exuberant winter arrangement of pine and spruce boughs includes dried wildflowers whose flowerheads have been spray-painted with a regular outdoor enamel. The red flowers are teasel, the gold are dwarf millet.

- Lovely colour is provided by berries (holly, cotoneaster, crabapple, firethorn, winterberry) and stems, including dogwood's red branches or the bright green of Japanese kerria.

- Buy small Christmas trees to flank the front steps — they can stay there all winter then be transplanted to another part of the garden or given away.

- Bittersweet vine or dried grape vines can be twisted over an obelisk. Or decorate the obelisk itself with more of those tiny glittery lights that look so welcoming in the cold dark of winter. Tuck evergreen boughs around the edges of the container.

- Take coloured lights off after the Christmas season, though white lights can stay in place. Keep the arrangements intact until it's time for your spring display.

ONE TO TRY

This combination is a perfect example of how stunning simplicity can be. The rounded shape of the plants, rising to a peak in the centre, balances the shape of the container nicely. For an instant lush look, choose plants in the largest pots available.

WHAT YOU'LL NEED

- a wide shallow container, about 45 cm (18 inches) across
- two to three miniature roses
- six to twelve pansies
- potting soil formulated for container growing, such as PC Magic Planter Soil

If your pot is larger or smaller than the one we've listed, adjust the number of plants accordingly.

1. Fill the container about two-thirds full of potting soil.
2. Carefully remove the roses from their pots and position them in the centre of the container. They shouldn't be positioned absolutely symmetrically — one could go in the centre with other two slightly off-centre from it.
3. Add more potting soil around the roses, covering them to the same height they were in the pot.
4. Fill in around the edges of the container with the pansies. Tuck a pansy plant or two between the roses so there will be a nice intermingling of the plants as they grow.
5. Add more potting soil around the pansies, firming it around the roots of all the plants.
6. Trim off any damaged leaves or flowers.
7. Water well.

CHANGING SEASONS

Pansies perform best in the cooler weather of spring and early summer. When they start to become leggy as the temperatures rise, replace them with six to twelve annual scaveola or trailing verbena, which will provide colour for the rest of the season.

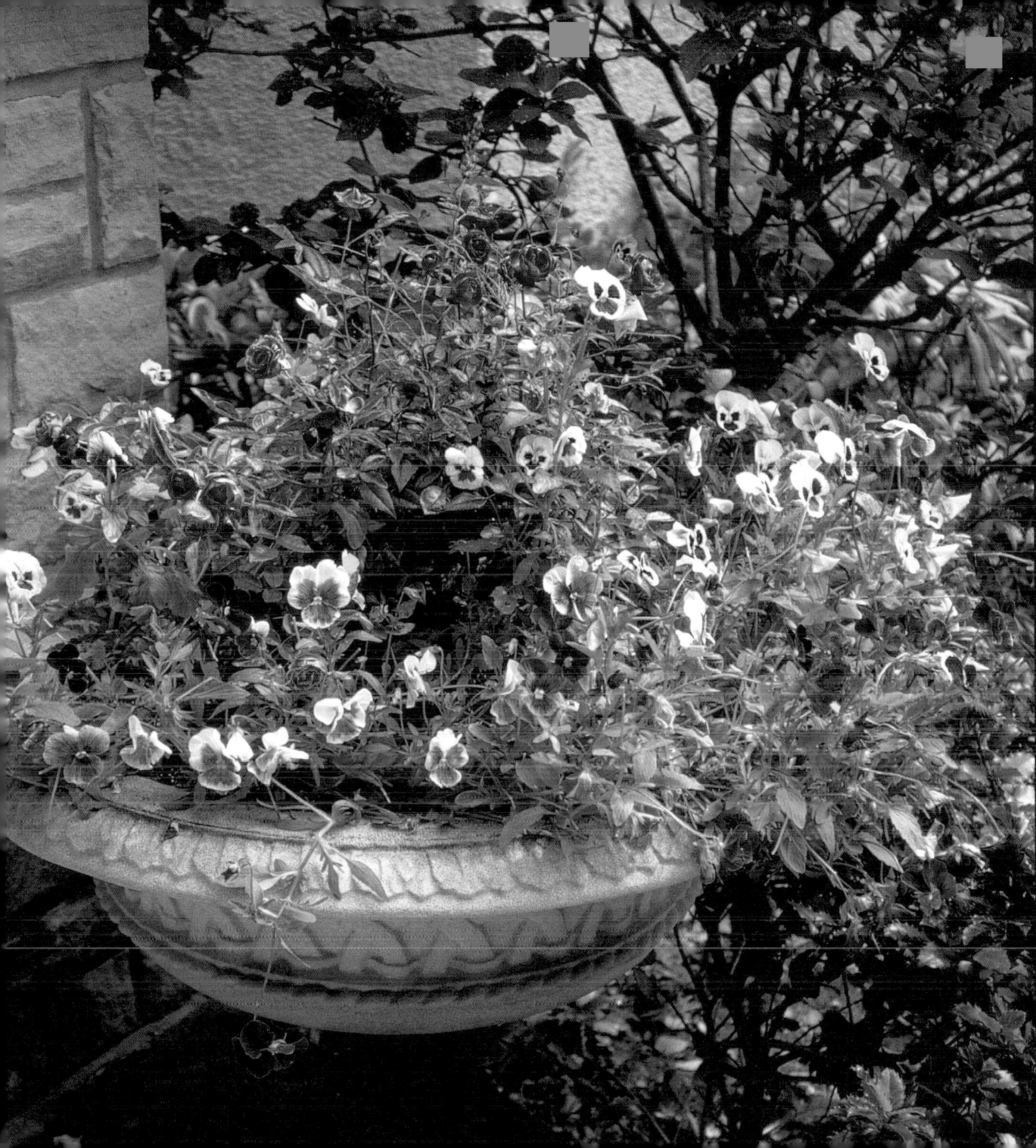

INDEX

ISBN: 0-9697259-5-7

Produced for Loblaws Inc. by Alpha Corporation/Susan Yates, Publisher
Written for Loblaws Inc. by Wendy Thomas
Landscape design consultant and horticultural expert: Janet Rosenberg
Photographs and horticultural editing: Janet Davis
Photographs by Sharon Kish: cover, 2, 10, 11, 43
Gardening maintenance specialist: Dale Winstanley
Copy editor: Greg Ioannou/Colborne Communications
Text and cover design: Dave Murphy/ArtPlus Ltd.
Page layout: Leanne Knox/ArtPlus Ltd.
Printed and bound in Canada by Kromar Printing

GARDEN DESIGN CREDITS

page 2: Dale Winstanley; page 3: Cookie Walton; page 5: urn by Cookie Walton, Garden by Janet Rosenberg & Associates; page 6: Allen Haskell; page 7: Zora Buchanan; page 9: Horticulture Design; page 10: Dale Winstanley; page 11: Janet Rosenberg & Associates; page 12: Bob Clark; page 14: Janet Rosenberg & Associates; page 16: Butchart Gardens; page 24: Janet Rosenberg & Associates; page 33: VanDusen Gardens; page 39 Katherine Frost, Southlands; page 47: Helene Morneau Environmentals; page 48: Clarissa Morawski; page 49: Horticulture Design; page 52: Casa Loma; page 53: Derek Bennett; page 54: Horticulture Design; page 59: Dianne Dietrich; page 58: Kevin Doyle; page 60: Perennial Gardens Corporation; page 61: Helga Ogilvie, A Touch of Green